Take A Deep Breath

From Calm to Chaos and Back Again

Julianna Langan

India | USA | UK

Copyright © Julianna Langan
All Rights Reserved.

This book has been self-published with all reasonable efforts taken to make the material error-free by the author. No part of this book shall be used, reproduced in any manner whatsoever without written permission from the author, except in the case of brief quotations embodied in critical articles and reviews.

The Author of this book is solely responsible and liable for its content including but not limited to the views, representations, descriptions, statements, information, opinions, and references ["Content"]. The Content of this book shall not constitute or be construed or deemed to reflect the opinion or expression of the Publisher or Editor. Neither the Publisher nor Editor endorse or approve the Content of this book or guarantee the reliability, accuracy, or completeness of the Content published herein and do not make any representations or warranties of any kind, express or implied, including but not limited to the implied warranties of merchantability, fitness for a particular purpose.

The Publisher and Editor shall not be liable whatsoever...

Made with ❤ on the BookLeaf Publishing Platform
www.bookleafpub.in
www.bookleafpub.com

Dedication

To Momma Bear,
who roared me forward when I froze,
who stood guard when the world felt too sharp,
who lent me her backbone when mine went soft,
who brewed strength in the same pot as her coffee,
and taught me that courage isn't always loud —
sometimes it's just showing up, again and again,
even when your hands shake.
Turns out, bravery runs in the family
(and yes, caffeine still flows in our veins).

And to Dad,
who said, "You wanted this, remember?" —
I do now.
Thanks for keeping me steady while she kept me strong.

Preface

This book began as a dare — not from anyone else, but from me.
I wanted to see if I could show up for myself every day,
to put a feeling into words,
even on the days when I didn't feel like I had any.
Each poem became a small act of proof:
that I could follow through,
that I could catch a mood before it slipped away,
that I could create something out of whatever the day handed me.
I didn't write these to be perfect.
I wrote them to be *honest*.
And somewhere between the good days and the hard ones,
I proved to myself that I could do it.

Acknowledgements

To my family — for cheering me on, even when I was too deep in my feelings to text back.

To my friends — thank you for pretending not to notice when I called my poems "drafts" for the tenth time.

To **Momma Bear**, for your endless encouragement (and occasional tough love). You're the reason I kept writing.

To **Dad**, for reminding me — over and over — that this was something I wanted, even when I forgot.

To everyone who ever asked, "How's the writing going?" — you might not have known it, but that question kept me accountable.

And finally, to the moods themselves — the good, the bad, and the dramatic — thank you for giving me something to write about every day.

1. The Leap

I have been on this cliff for years,
naming the wind, fearing the fall,
watching my words collect like feathers,
at my feet — soft, trembling,
never enough to build wings.

Every line I wrote hid behind me,
shy things, pressed between,
the ribs of old notebooks,
where no one could hear,
how loud they were trying to live.

But something changed —
maybe it was the quiet,
or how the moon kept whispering,
"You were born for this."

So here I am,
toes curled on the edge of my seat,
heart drumming against the unknown,

I take a breath —
and the fear turns into wind.

The fall becomes flight.
My words, at last,
become the sky.

2. Calm Before the Storm

The air holds its breath,
Everything stills —
the stars, the pulse in my throat,
even the doubts in the back of my mind
pause to listen.

It's the hush before the thunder,
the inhale before I jump.
My hands tremble,
but my soul —
she hums like lightning waiting to strike.

I can taste the storm coming,
that wild, holy kind if chaos
that happens when you finally choose
to trust yourself.

For a moment,
the world is made of silence and heartbeat.
and then —

I move.

The wind answers,
The clouds split open.
And then the calm that once held me
becomes the sound
of my own becoming.

3. A Reminder to Myself

For years,
I've been my own storm.
Every mirror a battlefield,
every word met with the whisper:
not enough.

I learned how to wear an apology,
I got tired of flinching
at my own reflection.
I realized that the voice that tore me down
was only scared of being seen.

So I spoke back — softly at first,
then louder, until the echo,
sounded like freedom.

Now I look at the scars
and call them evidence
that I lived through myself.

I am not my doubt.
I am the one that stayed.
The one who built a home
in the ruins of my own fear
and dared to love the view.

4. Learning to Love the Mirror

Some days,
I can't look at myself.
Not because I don recognize the face —
but because I do.
Every shadow, every scar,
every mistake stitched into my skin
like it never planned to leave.

I whisper apologies
to the person staring back,
but she doesn't always listen.
She's still angry
for all the times that I abandoned her
to please the world,
for every dream I buried
to make someone else comfortable.

Healing isn't pretty.
It's not one and done.

Its pulling the splinters out of the soul
one by one,
bleeding quietly,
hoping its worth it.

Some nights I still flinch
when I see my reflection —
the ghost of who I was
and the stranger I'm trying to become
meeting halfway.

But I'm learning.
To forgive.
To stay.
To look at the woman in the mirror
and not turn away.

And maybe someday,
I'll trace the cracks on her surface
and realize
they were never flaws —
just the places
where the light got in.

5. It's Okay

It's okay not to be okay.
To wake up and feel the weight of everything
before you even open your eyes.
To stare at the ceiling
and wonder how something so small as
BREATHING
can feel so heavy.

It's okay to be angry —
to let the fire in your chest
crackle and spit
without calling yourself ungrateful for the
burn.
Anger doesn't make you broken.
It means you're still fighting
for what matters.

It's okay to be overstimulated,
to want silence so deep
it feels like a hug.

To need space from the noise,
from the people,
from yourself.
You're not cold —
you're protecting your peace.

It's okay to have no energy.
To pause.
To rest.
To exist quietly without achieving a thing.
The world won't fall apart
because you stopped to breath.

You are allowed to be a storm one day
and a whisper the next.
You are allowed to be human.
And that, somehow,
is more than okay.

6. Becoming

Healing isn't a straight road.
It's a winding trail through memories
you swore you'd never revisit,
a dance between breaking and becoming
over and over again.

Some days it feels like the progress —
sunlight on your face,
breathing a little easier.
Other days, it's heavy,
like dragging your heart through the mud
and still calling it growth.

But healing isn't meant to be pretty.
It's meant to be *true*.
It's meant to strip away the noise
until the only voice left
is yours.

Because self-worth

isn't built from how they see you —
their opinions, their silence,
their love that came with conditions.
It's built from every moment
you chose to stay
when you wanted to disappear.

You are the one who defines your value,
You are the mirror
that matters most.

And one day,
you'll look at yourself and realize
that the journey -
the tears, the rage, the rebuilding -
It was about remembering
who you were all along.

7. Paper Worlds

When noise gets too loud,
I disappear between pages.
Ink becomes oxygen,
and the world I know
slowly fades into fiction.

I trade my skin for starlight,
my heartbeat for the rhythm of words,
Each sentence is a doorway,
each chapter a universe
that doesn't ask me to be anything
but curious.

In stories, I can breathe.
I can love without fear,
hurt without consequence,
live a thousand lives
without ever leaving my room.

The real world blurs —

but maybe that's okay.
Sometimes, the hearts just needs
a quieter kind of chaos,
a softer kind of truth.

When I close my book,
the spell lingers.
Reality waits — patient,
but changed somehow.
Because every story I enter
leaves fingerprints on my soul,
reminding me that escape isn't running away —
its finding pieces of myself
I forgot existed.

8. Still Standing

There are days
when quitting hums like a lullaby,
soft and tempting,
promising rest from the weight of it all.
And I almost listen.

But something inside me -
small, stubborn,
still alive -
refuses to let go.

Maybe it's hope.
Maybe it's spite.
Maybe it's the whisper that says,
You didn't come this far just to stop now.

The road is jagged,
the light flickers,
and sometimes I crawl
more than I walk.

But I move.
And that counts for something.

Because strength isn't loud.
It's quiet persistence.
It's standing back up
after the world tells you to stay down.

It's believing, even when belief
feels foolish.

I may bend,
I may break,
but I will not vanish.

The fire might dim -
but I am the one
who keeps it burning.

11. Too Much, Too Fast

It starts small.
A sound too loud,
a plan that shifts,
a word that lands wrong.
And suddenly,
it's all unraveling.

I try to breathe,
but the air feels crowded.
my chest tightens
over things that shouldn't matter,
but somehow they do.
somehow, they always do.

People say, *it's just a little thing,*
and maybe they're right —
but they don't see how one drop
can tip the glass
when it's already full.

I hate that I crumble this easy.
That a minor thing
can send me spiraling,
like I'm made of glass
and someone just whispered too loud.

It's exhausting
to live in a world
that keeps asking for calm
when your soul is built of thunder.

So I close my eyes.
Let the noise fade.
Remind myself
that overwhelmed doesn't mean weak —
it means I've been strong
for far too long
without resting.

And maybe that's okay.
Maybe this shaking
is just my body's way of saying,
please, slow down.

9. Heavy

I'm tired of fighting feelings
that never seem to end.
Tired of pretending I'm fine
when my soul feels threadbare
and my heart keeps whispering,
please, no more.

I'm tired of patching holes
in a ship that's already sinking,
of being the calm one,
the brave one,
the one who always finds the silver lining
even when I can't find myself.

I'm tired of forgiving storms
that never learned my name,
of carrying weight that isn't mine
just to prove I can.

Some nights,

I just want to set it all down --
the pain, the armor, the smile I wear for show--
and be allowed to fall apart without turning it into
poetry.

I don't want lessons tonight.
I don't want growth.
I just want to rest
and let the ache exist
without fixing it.

Because even warriors
need to stop swinging sometimes.
Even healers
need healing.

And I'm so tired
of always being both.

12. Music Keeps Me Afloat

People say, *it's just a little thing,*
and maybe they're right —
but they don't see how one drop
can tip the glass
when it's already full.

I hate that I crumble this easy.
That a minor thing
can send me spiraling,
like I'm made of glass
and someone just whispered too loud.

It's exhausting
to live in a world
that keeps asking for calm
when your soul is built of thunder.

So I close my eyes.
Let the noise fade.
Remind myself

that overwhelmed doesn't mean weak —
it means I've been strong
for far too long
without resting.

And maybe that's okay.
Maybe this shaking
is just my body's way of saying,
please, slow down."

I can feel it building again —
that pressure in my chest,
like the world's weight has found
a new place to rest.
My hands shake,
my breath stumbles,
and everything inside me
starts to crack.

But then —
a sound.
A note.
A voice that hums through the noise
like a hand finding mine in the dark.

The music slips in
where words can't reach,

soft at first,
then louder, steady,
like a heartbeat outside my own.

And suddenly I remember
how to breathe in rhythm again.
How to let the tears fall
without letting them drown me.

Every lyric feels like someone whispering,
I know. I've been there too.
Every chord wraps around the pieces of me
that were starting to come undone.

The world doesn't quiet —
not really —
but the chaos starts to sound
a little like melody.

So I stay.
Just long enough
to make it to the next song,
the next breath,
the next moment that doesn't hurt as much.

And maybe that's enough —
not peace, not perfection,

just the music
keeping me here.

10. The Edge of Still Here

Some nights,
I sit in the mirror and wonder
how many times a heart can break
and still remember how to beat.

There's a silence that feels heavy,
like the air before a scream.
I've been there --
that trembling space
between giving up and holding on.

It's not pretty.
It's not poetic.
It's just tired.
But somehow, tired still means alive.

I've learned that healing
isn't always soft.
Sometimes it's choosing to stay
one breath longer,

one heartbeat more,
even when it hurts to.
Especially then.

Hope doesn't always shine.
Sometimes it flickers,
like a match cupped in shaking hands --
small, scared,
but still burning.

And maybe thats enough for tonight:
not being okay,
but being *here.*
Still here.
Still trying.

13. For Now

Today, I look in the mirror
and don't flinch.
The light hits right,
the curve of my smile feels honest,
and for the first time in a while,
I don't search for what's wrong.

I know it won't last —
this peace is delicate,
a butterfly that lands
only when I stop chasing it.
Tomorrow, I might wake
and see someone else entirely —
someone smaller,
someone unsure.

But right now,
I see me.
Not the version I'm working toward,
not the one I wish I was —

just me,
soft edges and all.

And it's enough.
It's more than enough.

Because even if this confidence fades,
it means it existed once —
which means it can come back again.

So I smile,
memorizing the warmth in my own eyes,
and whisper to my reflection,
You did good today.

Then I walk away,
carrying that quiet pride
like sunlight in my pocket.

14. Becoming Gentle

For a long time,
I couldn't stand my own reflection.
Every glance felt like proof
that I was something unfixable —
a collection of flaws
stitched together by shame.

I'd stare at the mirror
until my own face blurred,
until all I could see
was everything I wasn't.
I thought beauty was something
other people carried easily,
while I had to earn it,
apologize for it,
fake it.

But healing snuck in quietly —
in the way my body carried me
even when I cursed it,

in the way my heart kept beating
after every heartbreak,
refusing to quit on me.

I started small:
a soft "thank you" in the mirror,
a hand resting gently on my own shoulder,
a promise to try again tomorrow.

And slowly,
the disgust began to loosen its grip.
I began to see the strength
beneath the skin I once despised.
I began to see someone worthy
of softness.

Now, when I look at myself,
I still see the scars —
but they don't sting like they used to.
They shine a little.
Like proof.

I'm not perfect.
I never will be.
But I'm learning that love
doesn't need perfection —
just patience.

And I've waited long enough
to finally be kind
to the person I am.

15. It's Not Your Fault

It's not your fault.
It never was.

It's not your fault
they didn't believe you,
that your truth
was too heavy for them to hold.
Some people fear
what they can't understand,
and they mistook your pain
for exaggeration,
your silence
for guilt.

It's not your fault
they blamed you —
for surviving,
for speaking,
for daring to remember.
You did nothing wrong

by trying to make sense
of what broke you.

You deserved gentleness,
not doubt.
You deserved arms
that held you,
not fingers
that pointed.

And I hope,
one day soon,
you stop carrying their disbelief
as if it belongs to you.

Because it doesn't.
It never did.

The truth still lives inside you,
unchanged by their denial.
You are still worthy
of peace,
of healing,
of being believed.

It's not your fault.
It never was.

16. The Weight Was Never Yours

They told you it was your fault.
Not with those words,
but with the silence that followed your truth.
With the way their eyes looked past you,
as if your pain was too loud
for their comfort.

You were young enough to believe them.
Old enough to carry it anyway.
So you learned to hold your breath,
to shrink your presence,
to apologize for wounds
you never gave yourself.

But none of it was yours.
The guilt, the shame, the stillness —
they were gifts you never asked for,
left on your doorstep

by people too afraid to look in the mirror.

You carried them anyway.
You made yourself smaller
to make room for their denial.
You buried your voice
because no one offered you an ear.

But listen now —
the ache in your chest isn't guilt.
It's grief.
Grief for the years you spent
believing you were the problem
when you were the proof.

Set it down, love.
The weight was never yours.
It never should've been.

17. They Called It a Lie

You told your story
and watched the words fall flat.
They didn't echo.
They didn't land.
They disappeared —
swallowed by disbelief
and the comfort of their own ignorance.

They called it a lie,
not because it wasn't true,
but because the truth
would've cracked the world
they built for themselves.

They needed you quiet.
They needed you small.
Because if they believed you,
they'd have to face the monsters
they let walk free.

But your truth didn't die that day.
It stayed inside you,
a stubborn ember
that refused to go out.

And maybe that's how courage grows —
not in the roar of belief,
but in the silence of being doubted,
and speaking anyway.

They called it a lie.
You called it survival.

And survival always wins.

18. Unlearning Guilt

I've spent years
saying "sorry" for things
I never did.

Sorry for taking up space.
Sorry for not healing fast enough.
Sorry for not pretending better.

Guilt taught me how to bend,
how to fold myself neatly
into the corners of other people's comfort.
But I am so tired
of shrinking into forgiveness
for things that weren't my fault.

Healing looks like rebellion now —
like standing tall
in the places I used to kneel.
It looks like saying,
I did nothing wrong.

And meaning it.

Some nights, I still forget.
Old habits whisper,
"you should've done more."
But guilt no longer gets
the final word.

I am unlearning the language
of blame.
Replacing it with
I survived.
I stayed.
I am enough.

And that's a truth
I'll never apologize for again.

19. If They Had Believed You

If they had believed you,
you might have healed sooner.
But maybe sooner
would've meant softer —
and you were built to be strong.

Their disbelief tried to cage you,
but it only sharpened your edges.
You grew in the dark,
roots wrapping around grief,
stretching toward light
you hadn't even seen yet.

You learned to be your own witness.
To validate the voice
they tried to erase.

If they had believed you,
you might have leaned on them.
Instead, you leaned on yourself —

and found out you could stand.

They took your innocence.
They doubted your truth.
But they couldn't touch
your becoming.

And that's the quiet revenge, isn't it?
You're still here.
You're still rising.
You believed you —
and that's what saved you.

20. The Mirror Learns to Listen

For years,
I couldn't look at myself
without flinching.

Every reflection was an accusation.
Every glance a reminder
of what they said I was.

But healing comes slow —
like sunrise after too many nights.
One morning,
I stood before the mirror
and said it out loud:
It happened.
And this time,
my reflection didn't look away.

The mirror learned to listen.
She didn't ask for proof.

She didn't doubt the tremor in my voice.
She simply stared back,
steady and kind,
as if to say,
I know. I was there too.

Now when I meet her eyes,
I see something like peace.
Not perfect —
but honest.
A fragile truce
between who I was
and who I'm still becoming.

The mirror believes me now.
And that, somehow,
feels like healing.

21. The Light That Stayed

There were days
you thought you'd never find it again —
that soft, stubborn light inside you.

They tried to convince you
it was gone,
that your truth was too ugly to glow.
But light doesn't need permission.
It doesn't ask to be believed.
It just burns.

Even when your voice shook,
even when your hope flickered,
something in you stayed lit.
You've carried that spark
through every dark room,
through every door that closed too soon.

And now, when you speak,
the words don't tremble.

They shine.
They say,
I was hurt,
but I am not ruined.
I was doubted,
but I am not erased.

You are the light that stayed.
The proof that truth survives
even when no one wants to hear it.

You don't need their belief anymore.
You only need your own.
And you have it now.
You have it.

www.ingramcontent.com/pod-product-compliance
Lightning Source LLC
Chambersburg PA
CBHW070500050426
42449CB00012B/3063